LANDSCAPING

Also by Joseph Allen

The Sound of Rooms (NPF Publications, 2000)
Night Patrol (Lapwing Publications, 2001)

LANDSCAPING

Joseph Allen

The Black Mountain Press

Acknowledgements

Some of these poems have appeared in the following publications:
*Billy Liar, The Black Mountain Review, Borderlines,
The Burning Bush, Cadenza, Coffee House, Dream Catcher,
Fortnight, Interchange, The Journal, Orbis, Other Poetry,
The Penniless Press, Poetry Cornwall, Poetry Ireland Review,
Poetry Scotland, The Reader, Reater, Rubella, Rustic Rub,
Seam, Various Artists, Working Titles, Yellow Crane.*

First published in the UK in 2003 by Flambard Press
Stable Cottage, East Fourstones, Hexham NE47 5DX
and Black Mountain Press
PO Box 9, Ballyclare, Northern Ireland BT39 0JW

Typeset by Harry Novak
Cover design by Gainford Design Associates
Printed in England by Cromwell Press, Trowbridge, Wiltshire

A CIP catalogue record for this book
is available from the British Library.
ISBN 1 873226 63 2
© 2003 Joseph Allen
All rights reserved

The publishers wish to thank Awards for All, Northern Ireland region
for financially supporting this publication.

Flambard Press wishes to thank Arts Council England, North East
for its financial support.

Website: www.flambardpress.co.uk

Contents

Landscaping	7
Epitaphs	8
No. 33	9
Stripping the Doors of Harryville Presbyterian Church	10
Judges	11
Hearing	12
Quiescent	13
Immortelle	14
Changes	15
May Day	16
Ecumenical	17
Learning	18
Labouring	19
The Shoot	20
Scars	21
Roaring Like a Lion	22
Water	23
Racavan Graveyard	24
Flying	25
Roads	26
Art Classes	27
Childhood	28
Transitions	29
Somewhere in Bourges	30
Legacy	31
Painters	32
Beaurainville	33
St Jude	34
The Game	35
Reflections	36

Borders	37
Crossing	38
Imaginary Germans	39
Young Socialists	40
A Wet Thursday Afternoon	41
Montreuil	42
The Foreman	43
Community Work	44
Travelling Blues	45
Touch	46
Leaving	47
Restoration	48
Gunfire	49
Returning	50
Festivities	51
Displacement	52
A Calm Sea	53
Planters	54
Haulage	55
Amsterdam	56
The Chosen Race	57
Heroes	58
Last Look	59
Interval	60
Pick-Up	61
Homesick	62
Transalpine Redemptorists	63
Gulag	64

Landscaping

Jimmy wakes to Karl
singing German folk songs,
lights a cigarette,
delaying the moment
when he must expose his flesh
to the cold air in the motor-home,
stepping over the remains
of last night's drink
to piss from the door
into the darkness of the lay-by.

Driving through endless Midland towns,
Karl praising the beauty
of the Bavarian villages,
telling stories of his childhood
in wartime Germany,
then stopping for the usual bacon, eggs and tea,
Karl asking directions – chatting up the waitress.

Arriving at another private house:
Karl marking out with lime
the dimensions for the tennis court
while Jimmy unloads the van,
starts to pick along the lines –
the routine work making the day pass quickly
finishing with the fading light.

Epitaphs

I came across some old photographs
holiday snapshots from our past,
you standing on a beach
young and slim in your swimsuit
me with long hair and first beard
looking straight into the camera
trying to be serious,
they reminded me of those summers
we spent together
caravanning in Cushendall
reading up on the stumpy tower
hours passed in the Layde graveyard
browsing over faded epitaphs
on fallen headstones,
visiting Dunluce in the rain
its ancient walls
indifferent,
you were afraid to cross Carrick-a-rede
I forcing myself
trying to impress,
having coffee and sandwiches
on the Giant's Causeway
we didn't feel like those others
who only came to gaze,
a part of this
would become a part of us
remind us of our early life together
now nothing but old photographs
I didn't even bother to throw away.

No. 33

Unexpectedly, I am reminded of you,
some small incident
from our past,
more vivid by its unimportance.

Once, you said suicides were born,
not made,
age was of no significance,
they fulfilled themselves
by completing the act.

Looking over old photographs
I find one of you as a child,
number 33 on a card
pinned to your Irish dancer's outfit,
standing to one side
apart from the others.

Is it my memory,
or has this distance
grown with the years?

Stripping the Doors of Harryville Presbyterian Church

Varnish peels in coils
from gently warming wood
the blowtorch
spreading a measured heat.

Three brothers
had passed these doors
in a regime of church
and Sunday School
long ceased before my birth.

Prayers in a front room
eyes defiantly open
on a face of piety,
resenting the intrusion.

And once, being interviewed
for a local garage,
an inability to name
our church minister
did me out of a job.

A smell of burnt wood,
sound of children
from the school opposite
interrupt my thoughts.

Judges

God cried out
from a grandfather's
stars-and-ladder tattoo.

Spoke from the burning bush
on Twelth Day banners.

My mother needed no mediator,
talked to her God
while cleaning house.

As a child, I wanted to be
one of Gideon's three hundred,
the sword arm of the Lord.

He speaks
from miniature Bibles
hidden in women's top knots.

Hearing

The confessional
of the hospital ward
binds us,
talk of families,
dances in parochial halls,
our operations.

The sinus cases
display their bandaged noses
my head swathed
like a balaclava
they tell me
how I took four hours
to come round.

We are a community,
sharing lemonade, sweets,
only with the priest's visit
is my difference
discovered.

Quiescent

The eve of his funeral,
we sit, quiet in our thoughts,
on the pigeon-loft steps.

Over the rooftops
the chapel tower stands black
against a pale pink
evening sky,
for him this summer
will not end.

No sound reaches us
from the street beyond,
all around is quiet,
as if muffled
by his silence.

Immortelle

Having a smoke
in the doorway,
heavy rain muffles
the sound of traffic
on the road.

In the winter, the boss would find work
around his house for the painters,
clearing gutters, sweeping leaves – odd jobs.

Today we are clearing rubbish
from his outhouses,
old furniture, clothing – family items
discarded throughout the years.

In an old chest
I find a collection of Victorian pornography,
grainy photographs of bodies
long returned to earth.

Changes

Six o'clock in the morning,
I walk to work
through the drizzling rain.

Beechfield Guest House,
Prospect Nursing Home,
all spacious gardens,
limes and copper beech.

The Grammar School,
built in 1828,
Tenax Propositi on the gates,
syringes round the entrance.

May Day

We parade the city streets,
tagging on behind
the May Day march,
trying to sell copies of *Militant*
to uninterested onlookers.

Feeling out of place
I walk among the Trotskyite banners
annoyed at letting myself
be talked into coming
suffering in the heat
the nausea of a hangover.

The parade scattering
as police move in to extract
a terrorist group
masquerading as civil-rights protesters,
our comrades calling to rally
at Transport House.

Ecumenical

We sit in chapel
unaccustomed to its ways.

Follow with a steady eye
the rise and fall
of the congregation.

Take our lead
from them.

We are not of your faith
but feel the loss.

Bear our awkwardness
like stigmata.

Learning

Teachers were mainly women,
middle-aged, without enthusiasm,
canes across the knuckles
of left-handed children
forcing them to conform.

Lunch times at my aunt's
bread toasted at an open fire,
sneaking up to the small
bedrooms overlooking the park,
their walls hung with Biblical paintings,
this burning bush, John the Baptist
seemed more real
than the stories from school.

One afternoon, as the sky darkened,
accompanied by rolls of thunder,
the teacher read to us
'The Lake Isle of Innisfree'
and for the first time
poetry became for me
more than a lesson.

Labouring

In winter we wear
extra jumpers, coats, balaclavas,
steel toecaps retain cold
like nothing else.

Pick work is best,
generating heat,
sting of wood on flesh
the only drawback.

I look at us,
broken, weatherbeaten,
huddled around fires
of wooden pallets, rubber tyres,
one might have seen us
in the Somme trenches,
Stalin's Gulags.

The Shoot

Walking to work across the fields
I watch the crows rising from the trees
and remember a November morning
my father took my friend and me
shooting for the first time.

We tripped sleepy-eyed
over the frost-hardened furrows
guns clasped to chests
my father striding ahead.

He told us to stand under the elms
and shoot among the rooks' nests –
as both guns fired
the scattering birds
covered us with droppings.

Scars

In his final illness
dependence
brought an intimacy
we had never known.

My awkward care
of an unfamiliar body,
his resentment of need.

Undressing him
for his bath
I notice for the first time
the identical scar
we carry on our right knees.

Roaring Like a Lion

In the newly erected
bandstand
Christians preach
sermons
to indifferent
shoppers.

Threats of damnation
hellfire
go unheeded
by passing sinners.

On the summerseats
the saved
with handbags
Sunday hats
listen for God
roaring like a lion
through the land.

Water

What was it
made you end your life –
some experience in your missionary work,
the depression
which haunted your schooldays?

And as you walked
deep into that cold water
did you recall those dark afternoons
in the music room,
at the piano beside Mr Cullen,
trying to master
Chopin's 'Raindrop' Prelude.

I remember you then
pale-faced, golden-haired,
incapable of violence,
until now.

Racavan Graveyard

Sitting in Racavan graveyard
enjoying the sunshine
I smoked a cigarette.

Restless,
I took a walk
along the lane
onto the road.

Rummaging through a derelict house
I found a volume of poetry
and a school exercise-book
once used by a Charles Foster.

Returning to the cemetery
I searched for his grave,
unable to find it
I thought of his children
maybe still alive
in America.

Flying

Winter kept us indoors,
hours spent on a dark stairwell,
we'd relieve our boredom
with leaps from the landing,
feet stinging on the floor below,
our future
an endless stretch of schooldays.

When your granny died
they gave me her bed,
hesitant at first
I grew accustomed to its use,
awakening once in the darkness
I was sure of
her weight on the mattress
beside me.

At your mother-in-law's funeral
I watched your embarrassment,
unable to cope with your wife's grief,
the unsure arm you placed on her shoulder.

Roads

The grave covered with leaves,
caw of rooks in the Autumn air,
the roads of your childhood
Bog, Craigadoo, Tully,
the melancholy clang
of rope on flagpole in the schoolyard.

Cycling to Saturday dance lessons,
drinking with friends,
set on your bike
by a sea of hands,
riding through the darkness.

Art Classes

Friday afternoon art classes,
he tried to interest us
in Cézanne or Gauguin,
we only had time for Dali,
feigning trips to the river to sketch,
lazing on the bank smoking.

Some days he would stay at his easle,
spotlight trained on the canvas,
mal stick steadying his hand
as he retouched old paintings,
talking about the permanence of art,
trying to explain Cézanne's obsession
with his mountain.

Years later I read his obituary,
tributes from the local vis-art society,
colleagues writing about
his contribution to art education,
and even still, when I see Cézanne's
Mont Sainte-Victoire, I am reminded of him.

Childhood

There is no hatred,
no desire for vengeance,
his draconian ways
seem petty now,
a father scoring victories
against his children.

Summers pass
and the voices in the yard
are gone
echoing down years of change.

The vacant chair
reverts to general use,
a presence ebbs,
no longer quiets
the conversation.

Transitions

Due to overcrowding,
our last year of primary school
was taught in a local church,
during lunch break
I would sneak into the main building,
wander among the pews
relishing the musty smell
of leather and old wood.

It was an uneasy year,
overshadowed by the prospect of change,
our move from the school grounds
seemed to us a premature severance,
marking us out as different.

And as we returned
from Christmas holidays,
the news of a classmate's drowning
left us somehow angry,
feeling as if he had escaped
our common destiny.

Somewhere in Bourges

Maria fries potato cakes
Alphonse pours Ricards,
from the radio
the sound of Moroccan folk music.

Tonight we have an invite,
a barbecue by the lake,
my guitar has been re-strung
for the occasion.

Tomorrow Johnie
starts his National Service –
the conversation is strained
avoiding the subject.

In the afternoon
Benny and Edouard arrive
bringing their guitar and violin,
we play Reinhardt and Grappelli
the air heavy with heat.

Legacy

The void of those years
you sealed
with your death.

The dead survive
in the living.

A knowledge of
past lives.

A passing
from one generation
to the next.

Your war medals
a legacy
rejected by us both.

Painters

Often we had lunch
at your house
in the street
where my mother was born,
your senile aunt
cursing about food
being taken from the table,
appealing to the Sacred Heart.

When we worked near my home
I would return the invite
knowing the strain
it would put on my mother's housekeeping.

Remember that job
we walked out on?
The Presbyterian minister's wife
refusing to let us use the toilet.

Beaurainville

I sit in the station café
watching old men
pour brandies into
their half-finished coffees.

Through the open door
the sound of lorries
being unloaded
for the morning market.

Having breakfast
while the villagers
wait to consult the doctor
in his back-room surgery.

Watching each one
leave their tables
and unfinished drinks
as their turn arrives.

Greeting neighbours
exchanging symptoms
occasionally glancing my way
whispering remarks to each other.

Paying my bill
I walk outside
across to the station
to await my train.

St Jude

Who gave onto you
these hopeless ones.

Many are they
who turn their face from you.

Call them now,
in despair they await.

Cry for them,
save each one
with your tears.

Listen for their voices,
speak your name.

The Game

With Summer
came a cricket of sorts,
fielders spread around
a macadamed playground.

Each boy trying
the impossible hit,
over the high back wall
to Scotch pines
and the park beyond.

Once, chasing a ricochet,
I ran the walled
passageway opposite,
almost hypnotised
by the heat and silence,
oblivious to the dream-like,
distant cries of ball, ball.

Reflections

Voices echoing from tiles,
smell of chlorine,
we bent over drawing-boards
rested on knees,
trying to capture patterns
made by reflections
of light on water,
bad copies of Hockney.

Later that year,
Christmas scenes
on the windows of the hospital,
the geriatric ward
unaccustomed to boyish voices,
we, oblivious of eyes
catching reflections of their youth.

Borders

Five years since I saw you last,
your English harder to understand
than your German girlfriend's,
you talked of unification,
how since the wall had come down
the West had been swamped
by East Germans and Turks –
with your shaven head
and combat trousers
you looked the perfect National Socialist.

You told me you were studying,
sitting college exams,
essential for career prospects,
how you and Anna
were planning marriage,
saving for a house,
and I thought of you back then,
the high school drop-out,
talking about freedom and travel.

Crossing

When she was widowed
she managed to keep the job,
living in the small cottage,
lifting the hand-operated barrier,
punctual for each train passing through,
the timetable kept in her head.

Each morning she would rise
to the same village routine
she had known since childhood,
her life rolled on
accompanied by the click
of wheels on track.

Until that morning
she lay with her lover,
the sound of splintering wood,
screeching of brakes,
as the eleven forty-five
crashed through the unopened crossing.

Imaginary Germans

The water was refreshing,
cool upon my skin
under the shading trees,
a welcome respite
from the sun,
lazily floating on my back
sudden splashes
an angry voice
laughter from the girls
on the river bank
as they explain
in broken English
the old man in his garden
is throwing bricks
at imaginary Germans.

Young Socialists

A wet Sunday,
dark enough to need a light
in the front room of the council house
where the Socialist Workers Party,
mainly unemployed,
hold their meetings.

I sit, nursing my hangover,
half listening to the same old discussions,
the Spanish Civil War, the Jarrow March,
swearing never to promise
to come again, no matter how drunk,
as we hand over our fifty pences
for the fighting fund.

And just as the guest speaker from Belfast
gets into full flow,
the secretary's senile mother
decides to clear the house,
the revolutionaries fleeing
as she accuses us of being terrorists.

A Wet Thursday Afternoon

Rain beats on the tarmac,
the senior nursing advisor
kneels in the wet
holes in the knees of her tights,
trying to resuscitate him –
she knows it's too late.

A powerfully built man,
the broad chest bared to the rain –
we cover the body
with an old coat from the security hut,
call the police.

The body can't be moved
until the police doctor arrives
and pronounces him dead –
the undertaker comes, and later,
shaking his head, a workmate removes the van.

Montreuil

Phillippe stands
behind the bar
smiling
arms folded
Danielle
takes orders.

A Parisian couple
on their annual
visit to relatives
an off-duty Gendarme
standing next to the drunk
he punched last night.

A long- distance lorry driver
trying to describe
his wife's ugliness
covers one side
of his face
with a hand.

Later he
drives through
the crash barriers
La Bamba
blaring on his radio.

The Foreman

He told me once
about sharing a bed
in digs in London,
how he kept moving away
as the boy pushed against him,
until, his back to the wall, he obliged,
no other way out he laughed.

Called his wife the budgie,
described how she arched her back
doing the crab,
getting excited as the other men
watched her skirt ride up.

Once, working in a quarry
hand-picking stones for building,
scrambling to safety from a landslide
I rushed back
pulling him clear
as he was struck by rocks.

Community Work

Drinking stout
in Mr O'Neill's,
watching football
on the TV,
keeping an eye out
for the foreman.

Sandwiches at ten o'clock
in Mrs McKeown's,
she complains
about her legs,
her son in England.

No answer at Mrs Devlin's:
wine bottle on the dresser,
Sacred Heart on the wall
above the body
on the carpet.

Travelling Blues

In the café Erich and Eva request Robert Johnson,
they tell me they are seeing Europe by bicycle,
Jean has just become a father,
invites us back to his place.

I show them my party-piece –
drinking a pint of wine down in one:
Jean phones the hospital to ask after his wife.

Next morning we laugh at my hangover,
how they carried me downstairs
arms outstretched like a crucifix,
yelling for my guitar.

Touch

Blind from birth
she went about her work
with confident familiarity,
setting the kettle to boil,
buttering scones and soda bread.

Finishing the strip of wallpaper
I was hanging,
I watched her pour
using her finger
on the cup's rim
to tell when it was full.

Looking in her Bible,
running my fingertips
over the Braille,
eyes closed,
attempting to understand.

Leaving

Sylvie is studying law
(her ticket to Paris or Lyon),
laughs when I tell her I like Morlaix –
you are a tourist, she says.

Tonight she tends the bar,
her parents at the cinema –
I keep her company,
drinking Ricard and water,
while she asks me about Ireland.

We stroll along the river,
Sylvie asks if I am ever homesick,
no, I tell her with a smile.

Restoration

Early morning,
winter,
the cold numbs my fingers
as I work,
old mortar crumbling
once new and strong
when someone before me
worked to build this church,
all that is left
is this tower,
the graveyard
where the congregation
lie quiet
unconscious of my work
to preserve the last remnant
of what they so proudly built.

Gunfire

Oppressive heat
shoulders burning
in the sun
as I paint
the church hall.

Behind me
the village
silent
dusty
in the afternoon.

The sound of shots
fired at the
unmanned police station
a car speeding past
the mark of
a ricocheted bullet
on the wall beside me.

Returning

Rain falls in Carantec
a cigarette
in a doorway,
waiting for the bus
to St Pol de Léon.

Leaving the café last night
lost my way in the dark
tried to sleep in a phone-box
kept awake by the cold
the intermittent beam
of a lighthouse
in the distance.

Half asleep on the bus
a ruined château
sitting off the road
the only thing in view
through the rain.

Festivities

Decorations are already shabby,
the whole lounge seems deflated,
staff from the benefits office
on their annual outing,
gin and tonics, hot whiskeys,
seasonal cigars,
building labourers with pints
of lager and stout,
trips to and from the bookies,
couples with untouched drinks
nothing to say,
drone of a singer
from wall speakers
and in the corner
a group of youths
are warned by the barman
to keep the laughter down.

Displacement

Gone, the town I was raised in,
red-brick mills and factories
have long given way
to middle-class houses, industrial estates,
the Victorian station and steam trains
replaced by an intercity terminal.

Roads once reserved for the rich
now lined with nursing homes,
the original triangular town centre
lost in a mess of shopping malls.

Even the castle ruins
have been cleared
to make way for a leisure complex
and the town's seven towers
are barely remembered,
my local accent
a puzzle to shop girls.

A Calm Sea

Walking along the shore
a storm
gathering out at sea,
ferry trying to dock.

Later awakened by shouts
sound of canvas
flapping in the wind.

Struggling with ropes
hammering in pegs,
Dutch girls
in shared misfortune.

Early morning,
debris strewn
across the campsite,
a calm sea.

Planters

In the early seventeenth century
the employees of Mercer's Livery Company
left their London homes,
took their families to Ireland,
settled in Movanagher.

Salmon and eel fisheries
on the nearby River Bann,
large medieval forests
providing fuel for kilns,
timber and brick transported
down river to Coleraine
for shipping to England.

The settlement abandoned
in the aftermath of the 1641 Rebellion,
three hundred and fifty years on
their ancestors still derisively referred
to as planters.

Haulage

Six days a week
he was away from home,
hauling loads of metal castings
to and from Dublin
along stretches of monotonous carriageway.

Missing his wife and young children,
hating the long hours,
the dried-up meals in cafés,
sleeping in lay-bys.

One night parked on the Dublin quays,
a girl he guessed to be about ten
climbed up on the hub of his lorry,
offered him sex for a fiver.

Amsterdam

Sitting in a café
in Amsterdam
talking blues
with a student
from Memphis.

He tells me
about his visit
to the Irish Bar
being told
to stay in at night
the city too dangerous
on your own.

Walking through
the red-light district
I overhear two tourists
leaving a peephole club
wishing they had found it
at the start of their stay.

The Chosen Race

Karl would use
a day spreading tarmac
as an excuse for a binge
cursing weak English lager
teaching me Bavarian drinking songs.

Drunk, he would fight with locals
arguing about the war
praising German soldiery
Aryan superiority.

Once he laughed and told me
how his father's battalion
were routed at the Somme
by a charge of Essex yeomanry
brandishing swords.

Heroes

Every year in primary school
lessons would stop
for an afternoon
as we children assembled
poppies for the British Legion,
green leaf and stem
connected to red petal
by a black plastic button.

Each Sunday afternoon
I watched television,
films such as *Khartoum*, *Zulu*,
my heroes were Gordon,
the men of Rorke's Drift.

History lessons brought me
Waterloo, the Crimea,
the Boer War and Somme,
connecting with local places
like Ladysmith Terrace, the Raglan Bar.

Once while working
in Kirkinriola graveyard
I came across the headstone
for one of Cromwell's captains
and at home photographs
of my father
from his time in the Inniskillens.

Last Look

The sky
heavy with rain
hung over Morlaix
as I, silent in thought,
watched the everyday
routine of the town.

Sitting on this bench
where in Summer
I enjoyed the shade
of those trees
now naked to my gaze.

Rising
I read a final time
the small memorial,
the Jewish names
of those
who years before
turned one last look
upon this square.

Interval

What remains in my memory
is not the music, dancing,
recital of poems at the feis,
the interior of the Protestant Hall,
but the novelty of a taxi ride home,
thunder and lightning

Time itself appears to stop,
the sound of birds,
passing cars, the tick of a clock
add to the stillness.

Pick-Up

Thinking himself
unobserved
he ambles across
the car park
under the windows
of the technical college
to the public toilets.

His cough
echoes around
the tiled walls
his eyes
scanning the open cubicles
alone
he lights a cigarette
and waits.

Homesick

A heatwave in Le Havre
I lounged around the campsite,
played my guitar.

This was your first time abroad,
a present for passing exams,
you felt awkward,
glad to hear English spoken.

We bought bottles of red wine,
you laughed at my French,
washed my hair
among giggling children.

At night we slept outdoors in the cool,
the nightman's flashlight
intermittent in the dark.

And that last night spent in Rouen,
you paid for a room
missing the comfort of a bed.

Transalpine Redemptorists

The Isle of Papa Stronsay
lies at the northern edge of Europe
where the Atlantic meets the North Sea.

Does the island's isolation
(Kirkwall, Orkney's capital,
is a ninety-minute ferry ride away)
remind them of their break from Rome,
refusing to stop the Mass in Latin.

In the near-perpetual
darkness of winter
do the voices of Picts
still echo across the sea-sprayed fields.

In the ruins of the eighth-century monastery
from the dry sandy soil
are dug pieces of porphyry
brought back from pilgrimages in the East
as a ritual object –

a thousand-year brown skeleton
found in the stone kist
buried under the site of the chapel.

Gulag

Mining camps in Norilsk,
two thousand miles north of Moscow,
nickel, cobalt, copper,
extracted from shafts
forty feet in the permafrost,
pick handles broken in half
to be of use in the confined space.

Men and women in silence
wearily return to the compound
and in the night
girls are dragged to the barracks,
met by visibly aroused guards.

In the early morning
the work squads pass
the frozen, naked bodies
dumped in the snow.